The Child's World®

Published by The Child's World®
1980 Lookout Drive • Mankato, MN 56003-1705
800-599-READ • www.childsworld.com

ACKNOWLEDGMENTS
The Child's World®: Mary Berendes, Publishing Director
The Design Lab: Design
Jody Jensen Shaffer: Editing
Pamela J. Mitsakos: Photo Research

PHOTO CREDITS
aspen rock/iStock.com: 17; gbh007/iStock.com: 21; Gordo25/iStock.com:
18; MaszaS/iStock.com: 22; mzoroyan/iStock.com: 14; Peter Hollander/
iStock.com: 13; Poznyakov/Shutterstock.com: cover, 1; R. Sherwood Veith/
iStock.com: 5; S.Borisov/Shutterstock.com: 6; Sophie Vigneault/www.123rf.
com: 9; tamaw/iStock.com: 10

ISBN 9781626870222
LCCN 2013947396

Printed in the United States of America in Mankato, Minnesota.
November 2013
PA02200

ABOUT THE AUTHORS

Cynthia Amoroso has worked as an elementary school teacher and a high school English teacher. Writing children's books is another way for her to share her passion for the written word.

Robert B. Noyed has worked as a newspaper reporter and in the communications department for a Minnesota school district. He enjoys the challenge and accomplishment of writing children's books.

Fall

BY CYNTHIA AMOROSO AND ROBERT B. NOYED

Fall is here! Fall is one of the four **seasons**. Another name for this season is **autumn**. Fall comes after summer and before winter.

Fall is the fourth season of the year.

In the fall, the sun **sets** earlier than it did in the summer. The air is warm during the day and cool at night.

Sunlight shining through fall leaves can be pretty.

The leaves on many trees change color. The leaves turn red, orange, yellow, and brown. Soon the leaves will drop from the trees.

Less sunlight makes leaves change color in the fall.

Farmers planted seeds in the spring. In the fall, their crops are ready to **harvest**.

This farmer is harvesting corn in October.

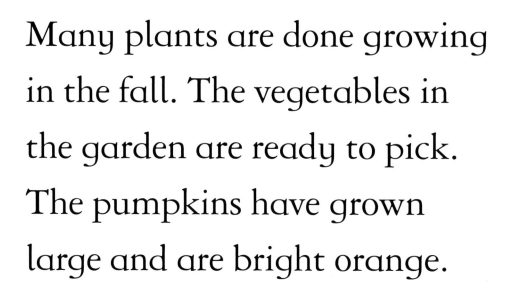

Many plants are done growing in the fall. The vegetables in the garden are ready to pick. The pumpkins have grown large and are bright orange.

Pumpkins can be used to make pies, breads, and cakes.

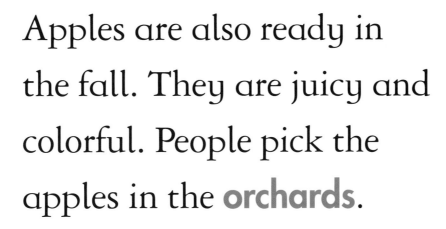

Apples are also ready in the fall. They are juicy and colorful. People pick the apples in the **orchards**.

Apple orchards often have many kinds of apples.

Fall is a busy time for many animals. They are getting ready for winter. Squirrels gather food to save for winter.

Squirrels, mice, and chipmunks are all animal relatives.

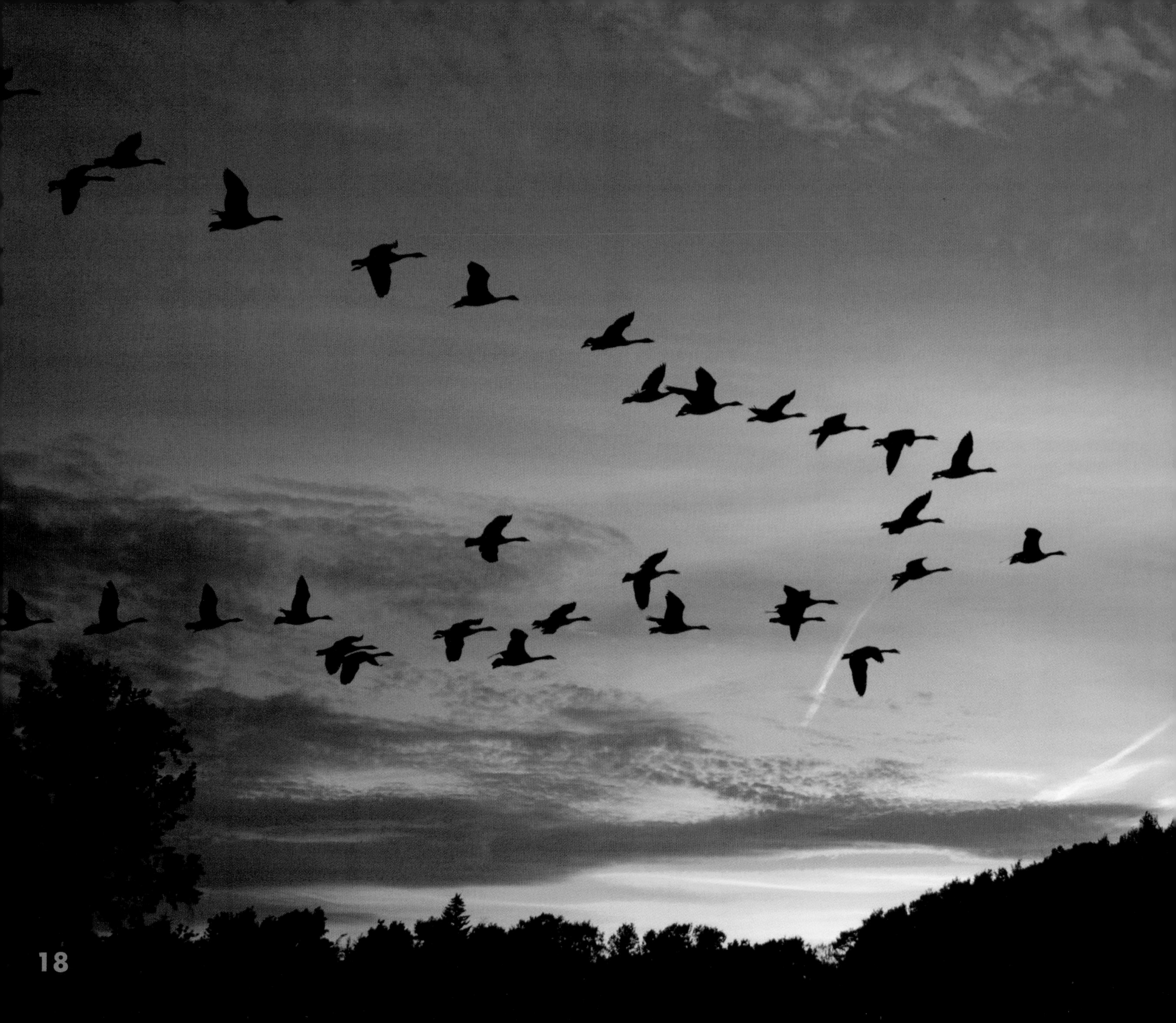

Many birds are in the sky in the fall. They are flying south for the winter. Some groups of birds make the shape of the letter V as they fly.

These geese are flying at sunset.

Leaves cover the ground.
Some people rake the leaves
into piles. Many children love
to jump into the leaves.

Jumping into leaves is fun!

The trees are brightly colored
in the fall. The air is crisp.
Enjoy the cool weather!

Warm clothes keep out fall's chilly air.

Glossary

autumn (AW-tum): Autumn is another name for fall. Autumn comes after summer.

harvest (HARV-ist): Harvest means to gather a crop on a farm. Farmers harvest in the fall.

orchards (OR-churdz): Orchards are farms where fruit grows. Apples grow in orchards.

seasons (SEE-zinz): Seasons are the four parts of the year. The four seasons are winter, spring, summer, and fall.

sets (SETS): The sun sets when it goes below the horizon. The sun sets earlier in the fall than in the summer.

To Find Out More

Books
Branley, Franklyn M. *Sunshine Makes the Seasons*. New York: HarperCollins, 2005.

Felix, Rebecca. *How's the Weather in Fall?* Ann Arbor, MI: Cherry Lake Pub., 2013.

Rockwell, Anne. *Four Seasons Make a Year*. New York: Walker & Co., 2004.

Web Sites
Visit our Web site for links about fall: *childsworld.com/links*

Note to Parents, Teachers, and Librarians: We routinely verify our Web links to make sure they are safe and active sites. So encourage your readers to check them out!

Index